A Vast and Ancient Wilderness

A VAST AND ANCIENT WILDERNESS *Images of the Great Basin*

BY CLAUDE FIDDLER

Edited by Steve Roper
Foreword by John Hart
Afterword by Michael Cohen

CHRONICLE BOOKS
SAN FRANCISCO

ACKNOWLEDGMENTS

Library of Congress Cataloging-in-Publication Data
    Fiddler, Claude.
    A vast and ancient wilderness : images of the Great Basin / by
Claude Fiddler ; edited by Steve Roper ; foreword by John Hart ;
afterword by Michael Cohen.
        120 pgs.   30.6 x 24.4 cm
        ISBN: 0-8118-1502-1 (hc)
        1. Great Basin—Pictorial works. 2. Great Basin—History. 3.
Natural history—Great Basin.   I. Roper, Steve.   II. Title.
        F789.F53   1997
        979—dc21   97-21313 CIP

Book and cover design by Sarah Bolles
Printed in Hong Kong.

Distributed in Canada by Raincoast Books
8680 Cambie Street
Vancouver, BC V6P 6M9

10 9 8 7 6 5 4 3 2 1

Chronicle Books
85 Second Street
San Francisco, CA 94105
Web Site: www.chronbooks.com

WITHOUT THE GENEROUS CONTRIBUTIONS from the following
individuals, the production of this book would not have been
possible. Heartfelt thanks go to Tom Rambo, Cathy Rose, Charles
Kilpatrick, Sam Mudie, Patty Glaser, Richard and Rosine Okie,
Bill and Judi Shupper, David Able, Julie Steinberg, and Victor
Diaz. You have all helped me to complete this rewarding project.

The science, technology, and expertise that together produce
a beautiful photograph are not to be underestimated. The following
companies and individuals provided the lab services, technical assis-
tance, and expertise that made the photographs and reproductions
for this book possible: Mark Robyn at Robyn Color, Matt Hesketh
and Rich Taylor at Photomation, Kim Kapin at A and I Color, and
John Wawrzonek at EverColor Fine Art.

Caroline Herter and Jeffrey Schulte at Chronicle Books
believed in the project and in the unique beauty of the Great Basin.
Without them, this book never would have been begun.

The writing for this book is the work of some eloquent and
inspired contemporary writers. It has been a great pleasure to work
with John Hart, Michael Cohen, and Steve Roper, who in addition
to writing the introduction also chose the quotations accompany-
ing the photographs.

Finally, my travel companions deserve to be mentioned for
putting up with thousands of highway miles, countless dirt roads,
mostly steep and trailless hikes, and the company of a somewhat
possessed photographer. Thanks for being there: Michael and Valerie
Cohen, Tim Snyder, Danny Whitmore, Nancy and Laurel Fiddler,
and especially my father, David Fiddler. Thank you Phyllis Benham
and Bruce Horn for cheerfully supplying your time and planes.

These people gave me more than I deserve. I can only hope
that this book serves as an adequate thank you to all of them.

CONTENTS

FOREWORD *John Hart*

I WAS DRIVING ACROSS the Great Basin with a companion unused to desert places. We were near the center of Nevada, on U.S. 50, east of the tiny town of Austin. We had crossed the massive Toiyabe Range, skirted the north end of the lofty Toquimas, and were approaching the escarpment of the Monitor Range, yet our view was much wider than it was high. I found myself talking nervously, defensively, about the steppe around us. "It's not all like this," I said, waving at miles of sagebrush. "Up in those ranges there are forests and streams. There are bristlecone pines on some of them, bristlecone groves you never hear about. There are meadows. Alpine lakes, even."

Then I stopped, for I'd caught myself breaking a promise made to myself long before not to misrepresent, not to sell short, one of my favorite regions of the world. It's true, of course, about the tarns and forests, the cirques and snowfields and ancient trees, but these bits of the Great Basin make up less than 1 percent of it. If you want alpine surroundings, you can probably find them closer to home.

People who love the Great Basin don't enjoy just the spots where it mimics the Sierra Nevada or the Rocky Mountains. They also like the endless, open piñon-juniper woodlands and the sage that, after a rainfall, gives off an odor as stirring as the wind off a glacier. They love the desert peach and the desert poppy and the bitterbrush and the Joshua tree, and even the drab, ubiquitous

6

rabbitbrush, with its pale, twisted leaves and yellow flowers. They know the lichen-splattered lava rims, the badlands with soils like drifts of powdered paint, the alkali pans with their dazzling, mathematical flatness. They've swum in the weird salt lakes with their heavy, amniotic water.

Perhaps Great Basin addicts are hooked most of all on the distance itself, the miles of nothing much. They like that it is hours between gas pumps; they understand that it can be days to a mechanic should your car break down. They know, too, that anyone you meet on one of those incredibly bad back roads will stop and lend a hand.

Heading out into the basin from one of the towns or cities that huddle around its flanks is almost like leaving a shoreline for a wild sea. Great Basin admirers are open to all of this: the strangeness, width, and cleanness of it all; the unsupportedness.

To love the Great Basin, you have to love it whole; and in this book, Claude Fiddler and Steve Roper show how that is done.

Claude Fiddler's photographs find the textures and the colors where the unpracticed eye might register only vacancy. Spend some time with images like these, and you'll never look at emptiness in quite the same way.

Steve Roper's lively history shows us the Great Basin as one of the continent's hard cases: a difficult habitat, even for the skillful Paiutes and Shoshones; for white explorers, a geographical puzzle that would not yield; for thousands of trekkers west in gold rush days, a debilitating obstacle. It wasn't really the Sierra Nevada that did in the Donner Party, Roper points out; it was the Great Basin.

This land was comprehended late. It was mapped late. It was settled late. And its subtle beauties were acknowledged very late in the game. Even the earth's polar regions found their interpreters, their lyrical defenders, before the Great Basin did.

After recognition (with a sometimes frightening lag) comes preservation. This phase also has been slow to arrive in the Great Basin region. Except in the California portion, the acreage devoted here to military purposes still dwarfs the acreage in parks and designated wilderness. Even where it appears to be unoccupied, this country tends to be used very hard. If it's not munitions, it's the results of mining: almost-random bulldozer scars, cavernous pits and strips, auriferous piles drizzled with cyanide. If not mining, in some regions it's off-the-road vehicles. If nothing else, it's grazing, often the excessive kind that punishes and impoverishes vegetation. (There should be lots more bunchgrass intermixed with that sagebrush than there is.) "The most common wilderness animal in the Great Basin," a conservationist wryly notes, "is the range cow."

We still have a long way to go toward embracing the Great Basin as a place worthy of respect, of celebration, and of some decent measure of protection. I'm grateful that Claude Fiddler and Steve Roper are helping so eloquently to get us there.

PREFACE   *Claude Fiddler*

ON A RECENT TRIP through Nevada, my dad reminded me of our long-ago family trips across what we referred to as "The Desert." I recall stopping in Elko for gas, an air of anxiety settling over the car. We filled the cooler to the brim with ice and sodas in anticipation of the searing heat that was certain to blast the family station wagon. What we mostly encountered, however, were fierce hailstorms and blizzards.

Interstate 80 was much lonelier in the early '60s, as were most of the Great Basin's byways, but now, as I make my way through the Basin, I can relate to my parents' trepidation and awe of this vast place. Signs proclaiming "Next Services 140 Miles" are enough to slam home the realization that I am out there, way out there, passing through 140 miles of basin and range, followed by more basin and range.

It was the distance, the loneliness, and the unique landscape that I was curious about when I took my first photographs of the Basin in 1987. What was it like in the middle of a vast, shimmering playa? What was in the depths of that canyon? What were the views from the crest of that ridge? What I found after traveling throughout the Great Basin was an enormous wilderness, one full of space that stretched for miles in every direction. In the grand space, it amazed me to discover deep erosion channels and standing water in the middle of playas, canyons that meandered for miles beneath thousand-foot walls, and twisted bristlecones surviving high on wind-blasted ridges.

The task of photographing an emptiness that was so full was exciting and satisfying, but the photography was not without its hardships. Miles and miles of dust and washboard roads often led to a precipitous four-wheel-drive climb that ultimately brought me to the end of the "driveable" track, and a rugged, dry hike. Sometimes I found myself battling strong, constant winds to take a photograph. In the end, the splendid isolation was usually worth the effort, and the promise of a private soak at a hot spring and an aromatic juniper campfire went a long way toward easing the pain of getting there.

Through this project, I have satisfied, in small measure, my curiosity about the landscape of the Great Basin. I know more about the place and its incredible beauty, but with this knowledge comes worry. Mary Austin called the Great Basin a "voiceless land," and along with this silence comes a certain vulnerability. Few people know the Basin, and therein lies danger. How many, if any, will know that a spring has dried up, causing the disappearance of a fish or snail species? Who will know when a rare plant is crushed under an ATV wheel, or when an annual stream is clandestinely piped to a cattle trough, thus destroying a riparian ecosystem?

This sly and immoral destruction of life and landscape might go largely unnoticed. My photographs do not depict the "man-mauled" desert of fellow photographer Richard Misrach. But I hope that, like Misrach's work, the photographs in this book will give the Great Basin a voice, a voice that I believe will ask for our care.

January 11, 1997
Crowley Lake, California

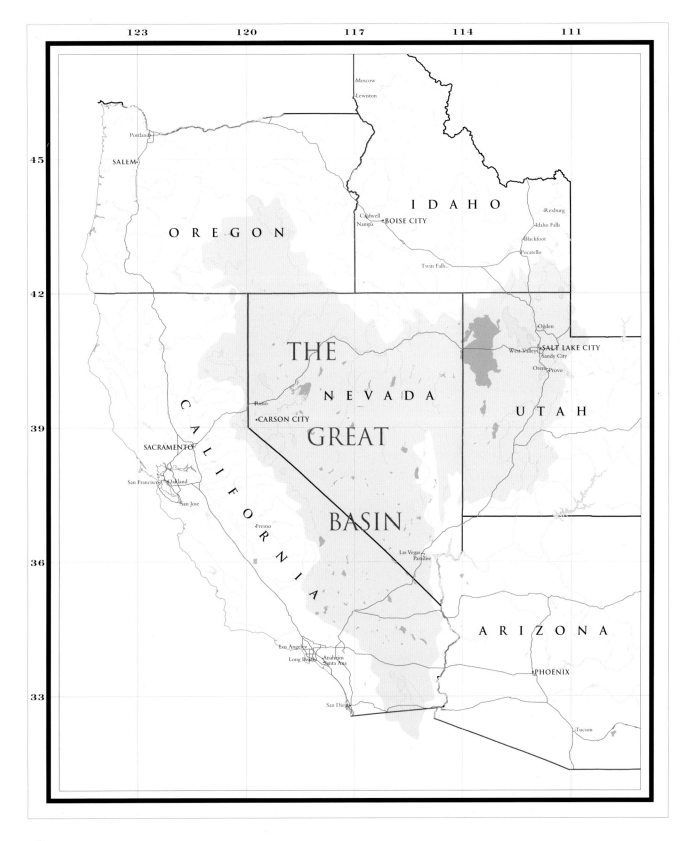

THE BLACK ROCK DESERT, NEVADA

AMERICA'S LOST QUARTER   *Steve Roper*

Traveling through the Great Basin, I have occasionally applauded the sentiment of the Englishman who, in a Nevada roadhouse a hundred years ago, was presented with a roasted sage grouse. Refusing this delicacy, he told the waiter, "Damn anything with wings that will stay in such a country."

Indeed, the Great Basin seems harsh, undone, inhospitable: America's lost quarter. Many travelers, both from the pioneer days and of the present, say it is a place to pass through quickly. There's a certain truth to this. I have cursed the endless alkali flats that shimmer at noon in August and feared the dust storms that spring up from nowhere, seek me out and pit my windshield, then move on to harass undernourished cattle whose ribs look as if they might break free at any moment. I have hunkered down in the false security of junipers as arctic winds packed needles of sleet into my ears. I have pondered my stupidity when my ancient Chevy Suburban, in need of a new clutch, chose to go on strike in the Black Rock Desert.

But the Great Basin has given me far more times of peace and silence than of trauma. Only there have I been taken back to an ancient time, to a place where nothing seems to change. It is not an intimate landscape. It is big and lonely and grand and Western; but what I appreciate most about it is its variety. Just when I decide the Basin is nothing but a desert, I look up at a mile-high escarpment of granite, with pines on the crest, tiny as matchsticks. Time for a walk. Sometimes, at the start of a hike, I'll spy a green-tailed towhee darting into a clump of rabbitbrush, savoring the heat and dryness. Six hours later, shivering at the base of an alpine snowfield, I might see a rosy-crowned finch snatching insects from the sun-cups. Such variety is typical of the Basin, and I never get tired of the contrast. Sagebrush to aspens, muddy wash to gem-clear brook, juniper to bristlecone—all beautiful, all altitude-dependent.

I've seen a herd of fifty antelope staring at me from atop a black lava flow. I've climbed peaks from which the view encompasses several thousand square miles of utter emptiness, without a single road visible. Once, within a graveyard of bristlecone pines, I found one snag so agonizingly beautiful that I couldn't keep my hands off it. Touching this solid, lifeless wood was not a meeting

with death; the snag had the feel of something immortal, like Carrara marble. Nearby, a weathered stone shelter occupied a small hillock. An Indian hunting lookout? A pioneer windbreak? Whatever it was, it fit perfectly with the landscape, and it will remain for centuries as is.

To be sure, the Great Basin is not all a silent wilderness. Salt Lake City, its satellites, and Reno are the only large cities within it, and Las Vegas lies just a few miles distant. Hundreds of other towns and hamlets dot the land, however. An interstate highway slices directly across the region, and a myriad of secondary and tertiary byways crisscross the area. Although you need these roads to get somewhere, it is easy to leave them and, an hour later, find yourself striding along a wash or a ridge or an ancient lake bed where no one has ever been before. Or at least it feels that way.

WHILE SEVERAL TECHNICAL definitions of the Great Basin exist, think of it as just that: a huge, shallow bowl. A saucer of 208,000 square miles, one-twentieth of the United States. It's a bowl because no water escapes to reach the ocean, a highly unusual state of affairs for such an enormous place. Because hundreds of mountain ranges lie inside this vast dish, you might never know you were in a basin, and in this sense the word is utterly inappropriate. Ridges and uplands, some two thousand miles of them, define the rim of the Great Basin, and this circumference, a circuit never even contemplated by hikers, includes both fourteen-thousand-foot peaks and modest hills that barely rise above the surrounding landscape. All the water captured within the Basin lies either in extensive shallow lakes, such as the Great Salt Lake, or in streams that either disappear into massive swamps or evaporate in alkaline flats.

To define the expanse of the Great Basin, one naturally begins with Nevada, since most of the state lies within it; but also included within its boundaries are a tiny chunk of Baja California, the Mojave Desert, an extremely long sliver of eastern California, southeastern Oregon, tidbits of Idaho and Wyoming, and Utah's western half. Heart-shaped, the Basin is extremely wide at the top, tapering down to a narrow point forty miles into Baja.

It is never easy to say what defines a mountain range, but geographer Alvin McLane has decreed that Nevada alone contains 314—and perhaps 600 dot the entire Great Basin. One is never out of sight of these uplifts. They jut out of flat deserts like battleships: the entire Pacific Fleet steaming north. There are no foothills here; these are young, raw mountains still being squeezed upward by forces far below their jagged summits. Although these ranges usually run north and south, they differ radically in length and elevation. A few miles from a long, high uplift one may well find a miniature outcrop tucked into the desert like an afterthought. Thirty-three ranges, heavily concentrated in central and eastern Nevada, contain summits higher than ten thousand feet. In several of these ranges— the Ruby Mountains and the Snake Range—you'll come across granite cliffs and alpine lakes where you might think you were in Colorado or the High Sierra. And below Wheeler Peak, in the Snake Range, you'll find a pocket glacier, the only such one in Nevada and not described until 1955.

The basins between the ranges are high themselves—about five thousand feet above sea level. The typical bottom-to-top relief is only about a vertical mile, but what a mile if you want to climb on foot to the ranges' summits! Forget the old thousand-feet-per-hour advice; these deceitful peaks will test your mettle. No step is easy, and when you check your altimeter watch after half a day of scrambling, thinking you must be close to the top, you will jiggle and curse the instrument even though you know it doesn't lie. The terrain is loose, rugged, and invariably complex. You'll find ridges with myriad sub-ridges; gullies that branch in exponential directions; drop-offs that scare you, then force detours; cliff bands that require half-mile traverses; and false summits that tease you unmercifully. Then you have the heat or, in winter, the nose-numbing winds. Add cactus and brush, and a dry stream bed where you thought you might find water, and you have a potential epic—even on a one-day outing.

FORTY MILLION YEARS AGO, intense volcanic activity ravaged the region that was to become the Great Basin. Massive ash falls blanketed the area, and pyroclastic gases swept through with regularity. Ash covered thousands of square miles, often to depths of hundreds of feet. Such activity continued for more than twenty million years, creating a grim, featureless landscape inhospitable to any form of life.

Then, about seventeen million years ago, as the various plates that make up the earth's crust off today's Pacific Coast began a new pattern of shifting, burrowing, and rotating, volcanism ceased and the devastated area began extending sideways. As it did, the thinning crust began to split and immense cracks (faults) formed in a north-south direction. Huge fault blocks slowly rose upward, sometimes tilting as they got top-heavy. Other sections of land collapsed. Over time, a basin-and-range landscape slowly developed, and it is still developing. The land continues to stretch apart—at a yard per century.

Mountain shaping also took place during this long period, for no sooner do mountains rise than erosion begins to tear them down. And where did all this material go? Down into the valleys between the ranges, of course. The valleys (or basins) of the Great Basin are simply huge trenches that have been filled in by the trillions of tons of debris shed by the mountains. Geologist Bill Fiero provides an arresting image in his *Geology of the Great Basin*:

"Some basins contain as much as ten thousand feet of late Cenozoic sediment. If the sediments were suddenly removed, the true relief of basin-and-range faulting would stand revealed. Some mountains in the Great Basin would tower from fifteen to twenty thousand feet above their adjacent bedrock floors. Whole mountain ranges lie buried in their detritus."

Although the Great Basin has looked much the same for the past four thousand years, the landscape changes subtly every day. Mountains shed rock; cattle graze the last of the native vegetation; gullies erode during summer thunderstorms; urbanization spreads. This is about all we can see in our puny life spans, but the geologic future looks grim. One day, if the stretching continues, much of the Great Basin will no longer be the land of interior drainage—and Winnemucca will be a seaport.

What fascinates me more than the ancient geology is the recent geomorphology, the configuration of the landscape. For instance, what is the story of those not-so-ancient inland seas whose "bathtub rings" are visible to this day?

About thirty-two thousand years ago, a gigantic lake began forming in the low-lying region where the Great Salt Lake now reposes. During the next seventeen-thousand years, Lake Bonneville, as we now call it, rose and fell intermittently. It stayed in equilibrium for centuries at a time, and when it did it created shoreline terraces—the bathtub rings. Overall, however, Lake Bonneville increased in size each millennium, finally covering most of northwest Utah. The ranges we now see west of Salt Lake City were islands, and the site of the future city lay a thousand feet below the lake's surface.

Then an event occurred that shows nature at its rawest, and what happened during the two- or three-month period that spelled doom to Lake Bonneville would have been a sight to watch—from a suitably high place. This cataclysm, which took place 14,500 years

ago, proved to be the biggest known flood, measured by volume, in all the earth's history. The geomorphic record reveals many details. Lake Bonneville, it seems, simply got too big; and at Red Rock Pass, just northeast of present-day Malad City, Idaho, the waters began spilling into the Snake River drainage to the north. At some point the weak rock forming the upper few hundred feet of the pass collapsed under the pressure, and Lake Bonneville exploded through this new gap at a rate of eighteen cubic miles a day. The lake dropped 340 feet and lost six thousand square miles of surface area before reverting to its former status as an inland sea. Since this cataclysmic event, the lake has continued shrinking, due to climatic changes, and today the shallow remnant we call the Great Salt Lake covers only one-tenth the area Bonneville did in its heyday. Because it's now relatively small and, once again, has no outlet, salts have accumulated in unimaginable quantities; the lake is seven times as salty as the ocean.

Lake Lahontan, yet another huge pluvial body of water, covered much of northwest Nevada. No cataclysm caused this 8,700-square-mile body of water to shrink; evaporation and climatic changes caused it to dry up almost completely ten thousand years ago. Pyramid and Walker Lakes are the most noteworthy remnants. The traveler who speeds southwest from Golconda along Interstate 80, then follows Highway 95 south to Hawthorne—a total of 210 miles—is traveling entirely along the floor of the old lake bed. That lake's surface would have been nine hundred feet above the sunroof.

When these huge lakes shrank, they often left immense, level regions called playas. The world-famous Bonneville Salt Flats, in far-western Utah, is the only one of these seen by the typical cross-country driver, but numerous other playas dot the Basin. These include Badwater, in Death Valley; the Alvord Desert, in the remote southeastern corner of Oregon; and the Black Rock Desert, north of Pyramid Lake. These blindingly white playas, the flattest locales on our planet, are also free of vegetation and surface rock, and this has allowed those obsessed with speed to use them to set world land records. After storms, playas can become lakes, but perhaps "mega-puddle" would be a better word for an immense body of water that is only a few inches deep.

THE FIRST INHABITANTS OF the Great Basin did not know much about its geologic record, but they knew how austere the region could be. By 11,500 years ago, the descendants of the wanderers who crossed the land bridge from Siberia to Alaska had spread throughout North America, coast to coast. We cannot know what they sought, but a good guess is that they wanted what most people do today: a benign climate where food is plentiful and enemies few, a place where life is relatively secure. The Great Basin was not the best region for this, with its lack of water and game; and the climate, then as now, presented harsh extremes. Still, a few nomadic tribes eked out a marginal existence in the Basin over the millennia, eating food such as rodents, grubs, and larvae that, though loaded with protein, hardly sound appetizing. Buffalo never ventured far into the arid regions, but pronghorn antelope were plentiful, if hard to hunt. Bighorn sheep were easier to track down, and even today one stumbles across ancient hunting blinds high on the sub-alpine ridgelines. To fill the protein gap when meat wasn't available, each fall the people would harvest bushels of pine nuts to eat during the long winter season.

Europeans came late to the Great Basin; the first one seems to have been Father Francisco Garcés, a Spanish missionary who trekked from Tucson to southern California in the spring of that momentous American year, 1776. Garcés passed through present-day Yuma, Arizona, and Needles, California, then somehow crossed the arid Mojave Desert to finally arrive at the uninhabited coastal site that soon would be called Los Angeles. Coincidentally, in late July of the same year, two other missionaries, Fathers Francisco Domínguez and Francisco Escalante, mounted an expedition from Santa Fe to try to find an easy route through uncharted Spanish territory to the coastal missions of California. Had they simply headed due west, they would have been fine; the route of legendary Highway 66—Albuquerque to Los Angeles—traverses gentle country compared to what lies just a few miles north. Instead, the party wandered north through Colorado and headed into what is now eastern Utah. In mid-September, the little band entered the Great Basin just south of the Great Salt Lake and turned south, encountering gentle terrain all the way to what is now Cedar City, Utah. Nine weeks had passed by that time, and the group realized that coastal California lay far, far to the west. With autumn snow covering the nearby peaks, the men knew it was time to head back toward Santa Fe.

HAD IT NOT BEEN FOR an Eastern fashion fad and a lust for a precious metal, the Great Basin might have remained untouched for a hundred years following the two tentative Spanish explorations. The plentiful supply of beavers and the lure of gold, however, assured that the region was fully known by the end of the nineteenth century.

In those long-ago days when men wore top hats, the most highly prized of all were made with the prime underfur of the beaver. Pressed into a tight, waterproof, and lustrous felt, the fur proved ideal. With beavers already decimated in the East, such hats commanded a stiff price, but after the Lewis and Clark Expedition of 1803–1806 it became known that the West had beavers galore. Within a few years, trappers—called "mountain men" for good reason—roamed the areas that were to become Colorado, Montana, and Wyoming. Often working alone, they had to be experts at surviving in their dangerous environment, one replete with mountainous terrain, harsh winters, occasionally hostile Indians, and the constant possibility of life-threatening injury. The names of several of these men—Jim Bridger, Kit Carson, and Jedediah Smith—are still well known today because books and movies have long portrayed these intrepid Americans as heroes.

By 1820, the West was shared by three nations, and every square mile of the land was in a state of political flux. Great Britain claimed the Oregon Country, that area west of the Continental Divide and north of the forty-second parallel (basically, present-day Washington, Oregon, and Idaho). Spain claimed present-day California, Nevada, Utah, Arizona, western Colorado, and most of New Mexico and Texas. And the United States, thanks to the Louisiana Purchase of 1803, owned virtually everything east of the Continental Divide except for Texas. The Indians, of course, were ignored as far as ownership went. This geopolitical situation might suggest potential trouble, but, in fact, surprisingly little friction took place between the three powers. Spain was mainly interested in California and the Southwest and it had, in 1790, relinquished most claims north of its settled southern regions. Furthermore, in the aftermath of the War of 1812, the United States and Britain had signed an agreement that provided for joint occupation of the Oregon Country. Without good maps or accurate means of measuring latitude and longitude, the trappers went about their business with little regard for borders, especially those around uninhabited Spanish territory (which became Mexican territory after that nation's independence in 1821).

By 1824, the trappers had ravaged the beaver population in the region surrounding the northeastern Great Basin, and so they began to penetrate the land of interior drainage, always seeking the magic stream sure to be overrun with beavers. There were rumors of such a river, and most maps of the day showed the Great Basin as a huge blank spot with a San Buenaventura River running from the Great Salt Lake to the Pacific. The trappers' movement into the region was fortuitous because, around this time, the Blackfoot Indians of Montana began to drive the mountain men southward. The Great Basin, essentially free of hostile tribes, seemed the best place to head for.

The two men most responsible for exploring the Great Basin in the 1820s were the American Jedediah Smith and the British-Canadian Peter Skene Ogden. The men and their expeditions (the former sponsored by the Hudson's Bay Company and the latter by the Rocky Mountain Fur Company) left Montana and entered the northeast corner of the Great Basin together, or perhaps a day apart, in late autumn 1824 via the Bear River. Cottonwoods lined this pleasant stream; the weather was tolerable, and the trapping was excellent. The two parties worked south and entered Mexican territory north of the Great Salt Lake in early May 1825, peacefully trapping along streams a few miles apart.

Meanwhile, a third group of trappers, of which Jim Bridger was a member, had also arrived in the Bear River area. Bridger, that same spring of 1825, appears to have followed the Bear River south to its terminus, the Great Salt Lake, thus becoming the first white man to sample the lake's water—and presumably to curse and spit it out. With the three groups summering near the present towns of Brigham City and Ogden, it's not surprising that friction developed. Ogden, in his terse, unpunctuated prose, wrote in his journal that "the Americans have taken nearly all the Beaver they are a Selfish Set they leave nothing for their Friends we act differently." In mid-May, the British and Americans had a heated but nonviolent disagreement about whose territory was whose, little realizing they were both in Mexican holdings. Ogden, a huge, strong man blessed with a moderate temper, retreated without rancor. After all, he had trapped 488 beavers in the previous four days and knew the region couldn't support many others.

By July 1826, all was forgiven and the trappers held their first Rendezvous near what is now Ogden. These famed summer gatherings, which lasted fourteen years, bracket the short era of the mountain men. Trappers, traders, and Indians—maybe eight hundred people all told—converged in a lush valley to sell furs, race ponies, gamble, buy supplies for the coming year, swap lies, form alliances, and generally have a good time. For some of the more solitary mountain men, this was the only real social contact of the year, and they made the best of it. Some married Indian women, and all-night parties, one gathers, were common. Fights broke out constantly, but as Washington Irving wrote in 1837, they often weren't too serious: "Having fought to their hearts' content, and been drubbed into a familiar acquaintance with each other's prowess and good qualities, they ended the fight by becoming firmer friends than they could have been rendered by a year's peaceable companionship."

After a week or two, most of the men were ready again for the solitude of their far-off environment. The traders headed back along the established routes to St. Louis with thousands of beaver pelts; the Indians, given whiskey and trinkets in exchange for the pelts they had brought in, faded back into the wilderness along with the trappers. All was quiet.

The first three Rendezvous were held in the Great Basin, along the Bear River or its tributaries; later ones were invariably located in western Wyoming, closer to St. Louis. As silk hats replaced beaver hats in the late 1830s, the trappers became as rare as the beavers, but during this splendid period the Great Basin was traversed several times.

Jedediah Smith was among the vanguard. Leaving the 1826 Rendezvous, located near present-day Hyrum, Utah, Smith headed off on a remarkable journey. Thinking that beavers could be found to the west, and the pelts perhaps shipped to California instead of to St. Louis (China was the world's largest fur-trading market), he set out on August 16 with fourteen companions on a long-term scouting trip. They first went south, following in the footsteps of the Domínguez-Escalante expedition. Then, from what is now St. George, Utah, they struck out into new territory, leaving the Great Basin and following the Virgin and Colorado Rivers to what is now the city of Needles. They were soon back in the Basin and the Mojave Desert, now following the half-century-old route of Father Garcés. In late November, they arrived at the mission of San Gabriel, just a few miles from present-day Los Angeles. The Mexican governor didn't like what he saw—fifteen grizzled, armed Americans, possibly spies—and ordered them to return the way they had come. Smith acquiesced and retreated eastward for a few days; then, apparently set on seeing where the fabled San Buenaventura River entered the Pacific, he disobeyed the governor and headed north up the San Joaquin Valley. If only he could find this river, he would presumably have an easy time following it back to the Great Salt Lake.

Winter turned into spring, and the San Buenaventura was nowhere to be found. Local Indians claimed that no rivers breached the great range to the east, and Smith finally came to believe this. Leaving all but two men behind in the Central Valley, he set out on May 20 across absolutely uncharted territory toward the Great Salt Lake. What followed was the first known crossing of the Sierra Nevada by nonnatives—and the first traverse of the full width of the Great Basin. Exactly where they crossed the range will never

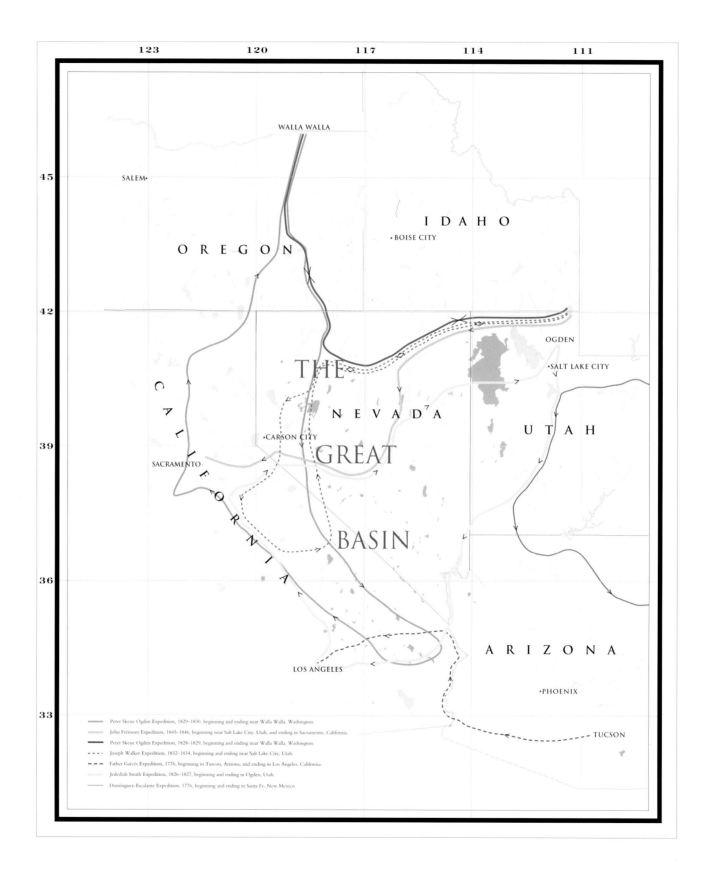

123   120   117   114   111

WALLA WALLA

45

SALEM•

I D A H O

• BOISE CITY

O R E G O N

42

THE

OGDEN

N E V A D A

•SALT LAKE CITY

U T A H

•CARSON CITY

39

SACRAMENTO

GREAT

BASIN

36

A R I Z O N A

LOS ANGELES

•PHOENIX

33

TUCSON

Peter Skene Ogden Expedition, 1829–1830, beginning and ending near Walla Walla, Washington.

John Frémont Expedition, 1845–1846, beginning near Salt Lake City, Utah, and ending in Sacramento, California.

Peter Skene Ogden Expedition, 1828–1829, beginning and ending near Walla Walla, Washington.

Joseph Walker Expedition, 1832–1834, beginning and ending near Salt Lake City, Utah.

Father Garcés Expedition, 1776, beginning in Tucson, Arizona, and ending in Los Angeles, California.

Jedediah Smith Expedition, 1826–1827, beginning and ending in Ogden, Utah.

Dominguez-Escalante Expedition, 1776, beginning and ending in Santa Fe, New Mexico.

be known, but Ebbetts Pass, not far north of Yosemite National Park, seems the most likely spot. The three explorers then descended into the rain shadow of the Sierra and began wandering across what are now Nevada and Utah, passing close by the features and sites that were to be named Walker Lake, Tonopah, Ely, Wheeler Peak, and Salt Lake City. On July 3, they arrived back at the 1827 Rendezvous, at Bear Lake (near the Idaho-Utah-Wyoming border), having been on the trail ten and a half months.

Though extremely little is known about Smith's dash across the center of the Great Basin, he left a short record of one bad scare, somewhere near the vast salt flats west of the Great Salt Lake. Low on water and eating unpalatable horse flesh, Smith thought the end was near: "It seemed possible and even probable we might perish in the desert unheard of and unpitied." Even though three men on horseback can move quickly, it's amazing that the Great Basin section of the journey, some 725 miles, was accomplished in only thirty-six days. How did the men circumvent the dozens of huge north-south ranges so effortlessly? Few travelers in the next three decades were able to move so efficiently.

PETER SKENE OGDEN WAS NOT IDLE during the late 1820s. If Jedediah Smith is most noted for having crossed the Great Basin west to east, then Ogden can be remembered for his discovery of the Humboldt River, later to be the main east-west conduit through Nevada to California, and his north to south traverse of the entire Basin. By 1828, Ogden knew the Oregon section of the Basin as well as any nonnative. Traveling from various outposts along the Columbia River, he made several forays into the lush Malheur Lake region and the Klamath River drainage, and he even dipped briefly into what is now the northeast corner of California. His two expeditions between 1828 and 1830 were even more dramatic.

Leaving Fort Nez Percé, on the Columbia River near the present town of Pasco, Washington, in late September 1828, Ogden and his party headed south to the familiar Malheur marshlands, pausing there to take advantage of the fabulous trapping. Then, having heard rumors of a large river to the south, they forged south past the Alvord Desert into new territory, entering Nevada not far to the west of present-day McDermitt. On November 9, near what would shortly be called Winnemucca, they became the first nonnatives to see the only major river of the Great Basin: the Humboldt, as we now call it. The course of this stream, which Ogden called the Unknown River, was a complete mystery, and he wondered if it could be the San Buenaventura. Realizing that winter was near, Ogden decided not to follow the stream west into unknown territory; instead he headed east to its source and pushed on toward present-day Pocatello, Idaho, by this time a traditional spot along the Snake River to hole up during the winter months.

The expedition reached the headwaters region of the Humboldt (as I will call it throughout to avoid confusion), east of modern-day Elko, in mid-December. A month later, the men had passed the Great Salt Lake, negotiated the Bear River watershed, and reached the Snake River encampment. They stayed here for only a short time before heading back to the Bear River, where they spent several weeks trapping the frigid streams.

The Humboldt obviously intrigued Ogden. What, he wondered, lay downstream from where he had abandoned it? Could this river be the long-sought avenue to the Pacific? Beaver heaven? In April, his little band returned to the Humboldt's headwaters, sometimes traveling thirty miles a day. A month passed as the men traveled down the river, making side trips to trap beavers in minor watersheds. Finally, near present-day Lovelock, a chagrined Ogden saw the river disappearing into an expansive marsh with no outlet. So much for the San Buenaventura! Ogden immediately changed the river's name from "Unknown" to "Swampy." He didn't know he had reached the end of the longest interior-drainage river on earth.

Six months later, after Odgen and his men had returned to Fort Nez Percé to deliver beaver pelts, he was heading south once again. It's difficult, after 170 years, to appreciate the lifestyle of the trappers. These rough, uneducated lads moved continually, with little pay and only a vague itinerary; without families nearby they were not tied to any one place. When the boss said, "Okay, fellows, we're leaving tomorrow," most of them must have cheered, like naive soldiers bursting to get into battle. The hardships were a given, and the idea of death both alien and unimportant. Most knew about the dangers of disease, injury, and Indians, but we can only assume that, like all youth, they felt invulnerable.

One wonders why an expedition into central Nevada would be mounted in winter, but Ogden and his group struck south from the Columbia in late October 1829, reaching the Humboldt's terminus, the swampy area now called the Humboldt Sink, sometime in December. They then headed into new territory, southward past what would soon be named Walker Lake. Somewhere near there, they crossed the by-now-invisible traces of Smith's small party of 1827 and continued southward. Since Ogden's journals were later lost in the Columbia River, we do not know exactly where his group went, but a vague itinerary is known. They continued south into the Mojave Desert, crossed it to reach California's Central Valley, and entered the Great Basin once again in the northeastern corner of the state. Then, still trapping, they headed toward the Columbia, reaching it in early July 1830. This ended Ogden's major expeditions, but his last is the most noteworthy, for he traversed the entire Basin north to south, a distance of nine hundred miles if one counts all the zigs and zags. This trip has probably never been repeated as Ogden and his men did it, on horseback and on foot.

THE 1830S WAS A CALM TIME in the Great Basin, with only one expedition of note visiting the region, the Bonneville-Walker party of 1832–1833. Benjamin Louis Eulaie de Bonneville, a captain in the United States Army, had grandiose plans for starting a trading empire in the West. Obtaining a long leave from the army, he headed out on a civilian expedition with Joseph Reddeford Walker, his second-in-command and his scout, and about sixty men. Upon arriving on the shores of the Great Salt Lake, Bonneville and a few dozen trappers headed north to the Snake River region, leaving vague instructions for Walker to explore to the west.

Walker and three dozen men headed for the Humboldt and followed it the entire 240 miles to its terminus, the swamp discovered by Ogden. Near there, on October 4, 1832, a tragedy occurred that would soon become commonplace in the West. Some Paiute Indians began stealing valuable traps from the streams, and two or three renegade trappers overreacted, murdering several suspected pilferers. About three hundred incensed Indians soon gathered around Walker's camp. Fearing more would come, and concerned about his men, he reluctantly gave the order to attack. Thirty Indians died. Zenas Leonard, clerk of the expedition, wrote that "the severity with which we dealt with these Indians may be revolting to the heart of the philanthropist; but the circumstances of the case altogether atone for the cruelty. It must be borne in mind that we were far removed from succor in case we were surrounded, and that the country we were in was swarming with hostile savages, sufficiently numerous to devour us." Walker had simply done what so many invaders do, which is to stride through the land with a swift sword, without regard for inhabitants they often see as subhuman.

Walker and his men continued west to the steep eastern flank of the Sierra, crossing the jutting range somewhere near present-day Bridgeport. On the way down the western flank, stumbling and starving, the group spied a great chasm with "mile-high waterfalls." This was Yosemite Valley, not to be seen again by nonnatives for eighteen years. A few days later they made yet another astonishing discovery, a grove of the gigantic trees now known as sequoias.

Months later, Walker and his group rounded the Sierra on its southern end, turned north, and once again arrived at the Humboldt Sink. And, once again, a conflict with the Paiutes erupted. The death tally this time: Indians fourteen, trappers none. The party pressed on, meeting an irate Bonneville in the Bear River drainage in early June 1834. "Who told you to waste a year going to California?" he said, in essence. Bonneville disappeared from the West soon thereafter; Walker's career had just begun.

THE TWO ONE-SIDED HUMBOLDT SINK massacres show all too well the deteriorating relations between Indians and nonnatives (and certainly show the superiority of bullets over arrows). The few tribes who attached themselves to the invaders, bringing in beaver and otter pelts in return for beads and whiskey, were tolerated—but they were the exceptions. Those who grudgingly admired some of the brave and colorful Plains tribes generally despised the Nevada Indians; according to various writers, they were naked, filthy, servile, treacherous, and not much advanced from animals. On an 1841 map a cartographer who felt compelled to write something across the huge blank area of the unknown Great Basin appended these words: "A few Indians are scattered over the plain, the most miserable objects in creation."

It's shocking today to read far more insensitive material, such as this 1844 passage from Charles Preuss: "Kit [Carson] bought an Indian boy of about twelve to fourteen years for forty dollars. He is to eat only raw meat, in order to get courage, says Kit, and in a few years he hopes to have trained him, with the Lord's help, so that he will at least be capable of stealing horses. He actually eats the raw marrow, with which Kit supplies him plentifully. He belongs to the Paiute Nation, which subsists only on mice, locusts, and roots, and such a life as the present must please him very much."

Mark Twain passed through the Great Basin on his way west in 1861, and his hyperbolic characterization of the Indians of the Nevada-Utah border can only make us cringe today. Of the Goshute tribe, he wrote, "[They were] hungry, always hungry, and yet never refusing anything that a hog would eat, though often eating what a hog would decline." They were also "savages who, when asked if they have the common Indian belief in a Great Spirit, show a something which almost amounts to emotion, thinking whiskey is referred to." A few paragraphs later, Twain apologized for being so insensitive: the Indians, he wrote, "have a hard enough time of it in the pitiless deserts." But his easy denigration is nevertheless a telling revelation of the deep-seated attitudes of the American newcomers.

Not surprisingly, given such racism, Indian-white relations deteriorated over the years, reaching a frenzied crescendo during the 1870s, when massacres, forced marches, and treaty infringements took place yearly. A decade later, the West was "won" and the Indians "subdued."

THE FUR TRADE TAPERED OFF by 1841, the year the Great Migration began. Some trappers, no longer young and with little to do, wandered eastward, thinking it might be time to start a family. As these men passed through small towns in the prairie states, they told their stories to local people and newspapers. A handful of books about the frontier also appeared, some written by trappers or expedition clerks. One can imagine that in a country fascinated with movement and the frontier, such books joggled the mind of many a would-be adventurer. The hook in all these tales and stories wasn't the Great Basin, of course; it was that paradise called California, in the words of one old trapper, a land of "perennial spring and boundless fertility." California was described as a place where the Indians were friendly and the Mexicans accommodating. Hundreds of thousands of Americans dreamed of this paradise.

Dreams are one thing, reality another. Of the five hundred Kansans who signed up to head west in 1841 from the tiny town of Weston, only sixty-nine showed up on the day of departure; yet this was still the beginning of the greatest voluntary human migration in history. About 165,000 people ended up in California during the ensuing two decades. Every one of these souls either walked, rode horseback, or traveled in covered wagons—usually a combination of the three—and each of them eventually had to face the rigors of the Great Basin.

As the emigrants in their wagon trains moved westward each spring for their 2,100-mile journey, hopes soared. California by early October! And, at first, all went well; the Great Plains region, mostly level, proved ideal for this type of travel. The pioneers could move swiftly along the Platte River and its northern branch for 470 miles. Wyoming, with the North Platte and Sweetwater Rivers forming a natural thoroughfare across two-thirds of the state, allowed equally easy progress. The Continental Divide, at South Pass, proved to be so gentle that until you came upon a stream flowing west it was impossible to know you were finally in the "real" West. But soon, inevitably, came the Great Basin, a nightmare by comparison.

Along large sections of the Great Basin, finding the next water was a constant concern. Since emigrants invariably crossed the Basin during August or September, the hottest time of year, water was life; but from year to year conditions were different, and advice from previous travelers often proved worthless. Those who rode on horseback across the land, as Jedediah Smith had done, could make an instant decision to head for the sure water at the base of a distant snowy range, perhaps at right angles to the intended route. But those who had to maneuver the heavy wagons, most often drawn by oxen, up and down gullies, around bluffs, through rock-studded gorges, and across thousands of sandy washes suffered discomfort and depression. Scouts on horseback headed out each day in advance of the party, but many pioneers arrived exhausted, after dark, to a campsite offering only a muddy, stagnant pool. Food proved to be another problem. The early travelers, thinking game abundant in the West, traveled light; but, as staples such as flour began to run out, a sense of desperation and even panic followed. Oxen tired and died, and abandoned wagons littered the landscape. Emigrant John Wood, writing in his diary in 1850, described the pioneers' mood as they contemplated the sere region west of present-day Lovelock: "All are preparing and dreading to cross [the Forty-Mile Desert], by far the worst desert we have met yet. They, perhaps, would not mind it, and neither would I, if we had plenty to eat; but here are hundreds already lamenting their anticipated death, and suffering on the burning plain. Expect to find the worst desert you ever saw and then find it worse than you expected." Wood at least maintained his sense of humor: "Our cattle are now getting so poor that it takes two to make a shadow."

Several "shortcuts" in eastern Nevada proved to be as arduous and as frightfully dry as the regular route—and even longer at times. The Donner Party, in the autumn of 1846, fell for one of these supposed time-savers and, far behind schedule already, made it to the snowy Sierra Nevada too late to cross. Their sad story—starvation, thirty-five deaths, and cannibalism—is well known.

Then came the discovery of gold in California. It's impossible to know what the migration would have been like without it. Would it have continued as a mere trickle? Would it have increased moderately each year? Word of the great lode discovered near Sacramento in January 1848 didn't affect the six hundred trekkers of that year; news traveled slowly back then. But the following year a stampede took place, and twenty-one thousand souls made the journey. Around seven hundred died, a dozen killed by Indians, the rest succumbing to cholera and accidents. Wagons ran over small children; people were badly burned by fires; and all too often firearms discharged accidentally (and sometimes not so accidentally).

Travelers who began early and moved efficiently in 1849 had an easy time, with plenty of fodder for their animals and no traffic jams at fords and narrow canyons. They progressed about twenty miles a day, taking perhaps one rest day out of every ten. But the emigrants who began late and moved slowly had a miserable time of it, enduring low rations, a shortage of fodder, and early snows. To add to their despair, they arrived in California twenty months after the discovery of gold, and few of the Forty-Niners ever picked up chunks of the precious metal from stream beds. Ironically, the non–Gold Rush "Forty-Eighters" stumbled onto the best claims and the untouched streams.

THE GREAT MIGRATION WAS NOT the only major Great Basin event of the 1840s: John Charles Frémont also roamed the region. This young army officer mounted four expeditions to the West during the decade of change, at the beginning of a career in which he was not only a noted Western explorer, but a man found guilty of disobeying an order by the most notorious court-martial in nineteenth-century America, California's first senator, the first Republican candidate for president, a Civil War general stationed far from the battlefields, and governor of the Arizona Territory. Late in his career he was referred to as the "Pathfinder," but in fact Frémont rarely explored new territory. Instead, his mission was to chart the land along the Oregon Trail and the California Trail (two-thirds of the overland route could be called by either name since, from Missouri to what is now Pocatello, Idaho, only one main route existed). Much of this territory was known in a general way by 1843, the year of Frémont's first venture into the Great Basin, but the motivation for some of the officer's wanderings may have come from his father-in-law, Thomas Hart Benton. This ultrapowerful Missouri senator, an expansionist with an unhealthy interest in Mexican holdings, cleared the way for Frémont's expeditions.

Frémont crisscrossed the West numerous times and visited the Great Basin twice. On his first trip, 1843–1844, the lieutenant and thirty-nine men followed the Oregon Trail west to present-day Portland, then trekked southeast to enter the Great Basin in far northwestern Nevada. As fall changed to winter, they proceeded south through the Black Rock Desert. Frémont's major "discovery" in the Basin on this journey was immense Pyramid Lake, near present-day Reno. There his party, low on rations, overindulged on the huge trout the local Paiutes had savored for centuries. (The Truckee River, the clear stream flowing into this lake, was originally named the Salmon Trout River by Frémont.) The lieutenant continued south, wandered about the Walker River drainage, then made a mad wintertime dash across the Sierra in the vicinity of the pass now named for his scout, Kit Carson.

Frémont made his next foray into the Great Basin in the autumn of 1845. His expedition split in two near present-day Elko, with Frémont, now a captain, and fifteen men heading south and southwest and Joseph Walker, that ubiquitous guide, continuing down the Humboldt (which Frémont named on this occasion). Walker had it easy, following, on horseback, a route that 150 emigrants had traveled with wagon trains just two months earlier. It could be argued that Frémont explored new territory for the next 325-odd miles; he apparently was unaware that he was closely following, in reverse, Jedediah Smith's eighteen-year-old route across central Nevada. It's impossible to know exactly where either party went, but it was certainly new ground to Frémont.

The two parties met at what is now Walker Lake late in the year, and once again they split up. Walker headed around the southern Sierra, while Frémont and fifteen men trekked north and exited the Great Basin at present-day Donner Summit, where that ill-fated party was to be stranded eleven months later. The captain continued into California, there to become intimately involved in the Bear Flag Revolt, part of the complex series of events that led to Mexico's ceding California to the United States in early 1848—nine days after gold had been discovered!

Frémont was hardly a true mountain man and undoubtedly wouldn't have lasted long alone in the wilderness. He traveled with a servant, always ate well (much better than his men, if we believe their stories), hired the finest scouts of the time, never had to deal with wagon trains and recalcitrant oxen, had strong and experienced young men under his command, and rarely trod untouched ground. But his accounts of his trips, published by the government and lavishly illustrated, ensured his fame within just a few years. He even got credit for finally debunking the San Buenaventura River myth. "There is no opening from [California] into the interior of the continent," he wrote in his journal on April 14, 1844. (Actually, Jedediah Smith had come to the same—but ignored—conclusion as he traveled up California's Central Valley in 1827.) The Pathfinder at least gets sole credit for two names that were to gain instant acceptance: the Golden Gate and the Great Basin.

THE EARLY 1850S MARKED the end of the "unknown" Great Basin. Expansionist congressmen in Washington had prevailed, and in 1848 a large portion of the British-held Pacific Northwest became the Oregon Territory, a part of the United States. With Mexico out of the picture, California was now a state and Utah a federal territory; near the Great Salt Lake the Mormons had a thriving colony underway as early as 1847. Emigrants traipsed across the desert each summer, and the 52,000 in 1852 alone was easily the largest voluntary migration in a single year in human history. Most made it through to the Golden State with a minimal amount of suffering, but hundreds died, mostly in the Great Basin. Thousands of abandoned wagons were used either as firewood or cannibalized for parts by subsequent travelers. (Even into the early 1940s, one could easily follow the ruts and trenches made by the wagons and collect wheels, remnants of yokes, and hauling chains. Solitary graves, marked by rotting wooden crosses whose inscriptions had long since been eroded by the elements, became curiosities. By today, however, most traces of the emigrants' passage through the Great Basin have disappeared, thanks to superhighways, off-road vehicles, urbanization, souvenir hunters, and the passage of time. Much more evidence exists in Wyoming and points east.)

By the early 1860s, when Horace Greeley and Mark Twain (and virtually all other Eastern travelers) were defaming Indians from their relatively comfortable stagecoaches, "tourist" travel across the Great Basin had become routine. Congress made Nevada a territory and then a state, and business ventures sprang up on the common crossing routes; most were small outposts, near water, that catered to hungry and thirsty horses and passengers. The most famous enterprise of all, the Pony Express, had transfer stations every ten to fifteen miles across the Basin, and mail reached California from St. Joseph, Missouri, in eight days—250 miles a day! After only eighteen months, this venture was doomed when telegraph lines spanned the continent. Surveyors crisscrossed the land, mapping the region. The railroad came next—crews hammered the Golden Spike into the final tie just north of the Great Salt Lake in 1869—and wealthy travelers could cross the Basin in a single day, playing poker and drinking whiskey in the club car, shuddering at the bleak and blurred vista outside when and if they glanced up.

BY THE BEGINNING OF THE TWENTIETH CENTURY a third of a million people called the Great Basin home. The vast majority were concentrated in the Salt Lake City region; Nevada's population was but 42,000. Mining and ranching formed the chief rural occupations, as they still do today, and life was slow paced. But with the advent of legalized gambling, in 1931, Nevada's population rocketed to the present 1.6 million. Growing twice as fast as any other state, Nevada is today a land of contrasts. Her largest cities share the problems of all metropolises—crime, pollution, and social tensions. Jeep tracks crisscross the fragile desert landscapes near the cities, and wheeling fighter jets constantly attest to the huge military presence. If you wish to see the real Great Basin, avoid the big cities.

Fortunately, much of the Great Basin remains a semi-wilderness, thanks in part to the United States government: 85 percent of Nevada is federally owned (mostly national forests and Bureau of Land Management land). Two national parks, Death Valley and Great Basin, offer the traveler extraordinary contrasts, and if you visited just these two reserves you'd come away with a near-complete picture of the Basin.

Can the words above and the photographs in this book really depict the Great Basin? Of course not. Claude Fiddler and I have latched onto an enormous subject and tried to make it compact, understandable, and eloquent. We hope the photographs will entice people to explore the Great Basin, for to appreciate it fully one must live there, walk its playas and pinyon-covered ridges, sleep out on a mountaintop and gaze at moonlit peaks sixty miles distant, listen to coyotes yipping and poorwills whistling. This book is hardly a substitute for knowing the region, and we hope you'll go out and see the land for yourself. Take your time; it's not love at first sight.

Images of the Great Basin

John Hart, 1996   [*from* STORM OVER MONO]

We are trained to expect big lakes to have green surroundings, a cool northern look. That beer-commercial freshness isn't here, and it takes a while to appreciate what is. A quick drive past Mono Lake in the hot, bright middle of the day may well leave you wondering what the fuss is all about. But if you hang around, be careful. In earliest morning, when the first light comes slanting in from Nevada; in midafternoon, when the sky grows lively with thunder-storms; in the evening, when sunset colors the spikes and ramparts of tufa; toward the end of summer, when the lake is alive with a million migratory birds; in winter, when snow lies to the waterline, you cannot stop and look without risk of being caught, of becoming what they call a Monophile.

ASPENS, EASTERN SIERRA NEVADA, CALIFORNIA

Mary Austin, 1903   [*from* THE LAND OF LITTLE RAIN]

Along springs and sunken watercourses one is surprised to find
such water-loving plants as grow widely in moist ground, but the
true desert breeds its own kind, each in its particular habitat. The
angle of a slope, the frontage of a hill, the structure of the soil
determines the plant. South-looking hills are nearly bare, and the
lower tree-line higher here by a thousand feet. Cañons running east
and west will have one wall naked and one clothed. Around dry
lakes and marshes the herbage preserves a set and orderly arrange-
ment. Most species have well-defined areas of growth, the best
index the voiceless land can give the traveler of his whereabouts.

John Muir, 1878   [*from* STEEP TRAILS]

When the traveller from California has crossed the Sierra and gone a little way down the eastern flank, the woods come to an end about as suddenly and completely as if, going westward, he had reached the ocean. From the very noblest forests in the world he emerges into free sunshine and dead alkaline lake-levels. Mountains are seen beyond, rising in bewildering abundance, range beyond range. But however closely we have been accustomed to associate forests and mountains, these always present a singularly barren aspect, appearing gray and forbidding and shadeless, like heaps of ashes dumped from the blazing sky.

Michael P. Cohen, 1996   [*from an unpublished manuscript*]

In the nineteenth century, Clarence Dutton described the ranges of the Great Basin as caterpillars crawling toward Mexico. Such a conception predates theories of plate tectonics, which explain everything and nothing, by turning the entire region into a succession of basins and oceans, of abysses opening and closing beneath islands of upturned stone. The idea that these many north- and south-tending ranges embody any linear chronology or direction is perhaps an illusion born of light and space, an illusion created by the flow of life upon them. When viewed from below and above, changes in weather and in the patterns of life make these mountains seem to move.

Colin Fletcher, 1964   [*from* THE THOUSAND-MILE SUMMER]

Living bristlecone pines are not impressive. They have none of the majesty of redwoods. A few reach seventy-five feet in height; but they are straggly, amorphous affairs. The majority never grow higher than thirty feet. . . . But the nobility of the dead trees transcends mere size. Every skeleton is a monument to age. From a squat nucleus that is less a dead tree trunk than an immense fossilized muscle there taper toward the sky a hundred anguished arms, smooth and suppliant and surrealist. The mellow brown wood, virtually indestructible under local conditions, is cracked into lines and knotted into pregnant curves. The eloquent dead live on among the silent living.

THE BRISTLECONES *Steve Roper, 1997*

THE WORD *FOREST* DOESN'T DESCRIBE a collection of bristlecone pines: *grove* is more appropriate—and *isolated grove* is even better. You'll never get lost wandering among the bristlecones. John Muir's favorite tree adjectives also don't readily apply to this species, which isn't really "noble" or "glorious." The young specimens are nice-looking pines, but the ancient ones, the ones we gravitate toward without thinking, are simply awesome, offering the finest display of weathered wood on earth.

Found only in the Great Basin and parts of Colorado, and only on two dozen mountain ranges, the bristlecones' most famous characteristic—incredible age—is a recent discovery. As late as 1950, little was known about the tree or its range; and virtually nothing about its age. Several reasons account for this lack of knowledge. Their location, high atop remote desert ranges, kept them far removed from casual visitors. Few maintained trails existed, so only hardy hunters and prospectors ever saw the trees. And these outdoorsmen, like many other folk, could hardly have told the subtle difference between a bristlecone and a limber pine, a far more common timberline tree. But in early 1958 Edmund Schulman, a dendrochronologist (one who analyzes climate changes by looking at tree rings), informed the world through the *National Geographic*

that some of these trees were 4,600 years old. Later research has added another four hundred years to this figure.

Drive up into California's White Mountains, park, and walk into a grove of bristlecones. The first thing you'll notice is that you'll probably be breathing rather hard; the trees grow mainly at elevations between 9,500 and 11,800 feet. Make your way across the white, rocky "soil" to what appears to be a lifeless tree, one distinguished by its furrowed, golden trunk and the dozens of naked snags that jut up into the deep blue sky. Dead as a doornail. Then you spy a single branch that sports lush green needles and even a few cones. At first this seems to be a mistake, and you look around for a healthier, close-by tree that has sent a branch into this one's territory. Then you look again and follow the living part of the tree downward. A narrow, curving strip of bark is plastered against the trunk, snaking down to the ground in anything but a direct manner. In this unbelievably dry, cold, and windy environment, with few nutrients, this tree has sacrificed much of itself in order that a limb might live. These strip-bark trees, by definition more than fifteen hundred years old, rise all around you, once you have taken the time to look. It's a revelation to stand among these sentinels; you're seeing an example of perfect adaptation.

FALL COLOR ALONG ROCK CREEK, CALIFORNIA

John Muir, 1878   [*from* STEEP TRAILS]

We passed through a magnificent grove of aspens, about a hundred acres in extent, through which the mellow sunshine sifted in ravishing splendor, showing every leaf to be as beautiful in color as the wing of a butterfly, and making them tell gloriously against the evergreens. These extensive groves of aspen are a marked feature of the . . . woods. Some of the lower mountains are covered with them, giving rise to remarkably beautiful effects in general views— waving, trembling masses of pale, translucent green in spring and summer, yellow and orange in autumn, while in winter, after every leaf has fallen, the white bark of the boles and branches seen in mass seems like a cloud of mist.

Solomon Nunes Carvalho, 1857   [*from* INCIDENTS OF TRAVELS]

In travelling over the vast prairies and mountains it is well that the range of our vision has certain limits. If we could take within scope of our sight, the whole extent of the distance to be travelled, we should most probably give up the original intention as one of the impossibilities; a wise Providence has ordained otherwise. The distance is bounded frequently by high ranges of mountains, which cut off the perspective, or the atmosphere between the eye and the object produces an aerial effect, which obscures like a curtain, the far spread waste, inspiring the wearied traveller with fresh and renewed energy.

Israel C. Russell, 1889   [*from* QUARTERNARY HISTORY OF THE MONO VALLEY]

In the middle distance there rests upon the desert plain what
appears to be a wide sheet of burnished metal, so even and brilliant
is its surface. It is Lake Mono. At times the waters reflect the mountains beyond with strange distinctness and impress one as being in
some way peculiar, but usually their ripples gleam and flash in the
sunlight like the waves of ordinary lakes. No one would think from
a distant view that the water which seems so bright and enticing
is in reality so dense and alkaline that it would quickly cause the
death of a traveler who could find no other with which to quench
his thirst. It is in truth a Dead Sea, but without the mysterious
charm that history, tradition, and religion impart to the similar sea
in Palestine.

John Muir, 1878   [*from* STEEP TRAILS]

Making your way along any of the wide gray valleys that stretch from north to south, seldom will your eye be interrupted by a single mark of cultivation. The smooth lake-like ground sweeps on indefinitely, growing more and more dim in the glowing sunshine, while a mountain-range from eight to ten thousand feet high bounds the view on either hand. No singing water, no green sod, no moist nook to rest in—mountain and valley alike naked and shadowless in the sun-glare; and though, perhaps, travelling a well-worn road to a gold or silver mine, and supplied with repeated instructions, you can scarce hope to find any human habitation from day to day, so vast and impressive is the hot, dusty, alkaline wildness.

Thomas H. Means, 1932   [*from the* 1932 SIERRA CLUB BULLETIN]

The brilliant colors stand out vividly in the clear air; distances are deceptive. The colors change with the light; they are fleeting, and the despair of artists who try to put them on canvas. The light is strong, and the inexperienced photographer is likely to overexpose pictures. The overlying blue of the full daylight changes to purple in the evening, and the shadows become deep purple to black. The rough contours become soft as the sun descends, and the scene takes on a mystical hue and brings thoughts of the Arabian Nights. Maxfield Parrish must have derived some of his color technique from the desert.

Mary Austin, 1903   [*from* THE LAND OF LITTLE RAIN]

You may come into the borders of [the Great Basin] from the south
by a stage journey that has the effect of involving a great lapse of
time, or from the north by rail, dropping out of the overland route
at Reno. The best of all ways is over the Sierra passes by pack and
trail, seeing and believing. But the real heart and core of the country are not to be come at in a month's vacation. One must summer
and winter with the land and wait its occasions. Pine woods that
take two and three seasons to the ripening of cones, roots that lie by
in the sand seven years awaiting a growing rain, firs that grow fifty
years before flowering—these do not scrape acquaintance.

THE NAMES   *Steve Roper, 1997*

MAYBE THE GREAT BASIN doesn't have a monopoly on strange and interesting place-names, but thanks to its variety of landscapes, its mining history, and some imaginative namers, it manages quite well. The stories behind many names are either obvious (Bald Mountain, of which there are at least eleven in Nevada, with variations) or lost in the ether of time (Beer Bottle Pass and Poker Brown Gap).

What to make of Buster-Jangle Crater? Yet what a fine name compared to the much better known Lunar Crater, a name given to a similar feature by someone with the imagination of a desert tortoise. What celebration or remembrance sparked Auld Lang Syne Peak? What ignorant bird-watcher named the Nightingale Mountains? Or was this range named in honor of Florence, the nurse, after the Crimean War? Neither, it turns out: the name's a corruption of the name of an early soldier, Captain Nightengill.

We can see the pioneer influence behind Wagon Tire Mountain, Fencemaker Pass, Robber Roost Hills, and Horsethief Mountain. Much later we have the Fallout Hills, near the atomic bomb test site, and this sadly and forever reminds us of our midcentury folly.

Some names might have been given by hallucinating travelers on their last legs. White Elephant Butte. Iron Blossom Mountain. Mirage. God's Pocket Peak. Blue Eagle Springs. King Lear Peak.

Perhaps a pioneer cook thought of Baking Powder Flat; surely no scout or hunter would have risked his reputation by so naming it. Somebody versed in both Latin and mining must have named Argenta Point; other, more prosaic, miners identified Mineral Hill, Silverado Mountain, and Gold Hill, Goldbanks Hills, Goldbud, Gold Point, Goldfield. Hunters and/or red-meat-satiated pioneers gave offerings to the gods: Stag Mountain, Antelope Mountain, perhaps even Porcupine Mountain. And what horror took place in the town called Ursine?

Everyone was from out-of-state in the pioneer days, and many must have been homesick. New Boston. Portuguese Mountain. Devon Peak. Calcutta Lake. I see a traveler from India traversing the desert in 1890, eager to name something after her nation's crowded, humid capital, but having lots of trouble. There's probably a simpler explanation.

Finally, we come to banality. No one, I hope, will spring forth to claim these names. Desert Range. Desert Valley. Black Mountain (a dozen of these). Granite Mountain. White Rock. Jack Creek. Cold Springs. Warm Springs. We can do better.

Dan DeQuille, 1861   [from WASHOE RAMBLES]

Before us, to the northward, miles on miles away, lay spread out the most magnificent panorama of mountain scenery ever seen or conceived of. No pen could do justice to this symmetrical chaos of peaks! Were I to write for a month, I could not convey to the reader more than a faint, uncertain notion of that appearance of lightness, yet overwhelming conviction of massiveness and solidity, observed and *felt* in standing before those mountains, that seem to sit so lightly in the laps of mountains, and those hills that skip and roll at their feet! What artist, with pencil and gross, material pigments, dare venture to sit down before this concourse of hills to paint their portraits, and not blush at his miserable, lifeless caricatures—his stark dead, canvass-and-ochre peaks?

Elmo Robinson, 1938   [*from the* 1938 SIERRA CLUB BULLETIN]

Parts of the earth's crust that were once regarded as at least uninteresting, or more probably as ugly, repelling, and inimical, are now looked upon as bits of marvelous beauty, inviting and friendly. From horror to "agreeable horror" to agreeableness without horror, to fascinated delight—such has been our heritage of attitudes.

John C. Frémont, 1844   [*from* REPORT OF THE EXPLORING EXPEDITION]

Beyond, a defile between the mountains descended rapidly about two thousand feet; and, filling up all the lower space, was a sheet of green water, some twenty miles broad. It broke upon our eyes like the ocean. The neighboring peaks rose high above us, and we ascended one of them to obtain a better view. The waves were curling in the breeze, and their dark-green color showed it to be a body of deep water. For a long time we sat enjoying the view, for we had become fatigued with mountains, and the free expanse of moving waves was very grateful. It was set like a gem in the mountains, which, from our position, seemed to enclose it almost entirely.

STORM OVER PYRAMID LAKE, NEVADA

Dan DeQuille, 1861   [*from* WASHOE RAMBLES]

We are standing far, far out in a desert. It is hot, *very hot*. The earth is hot. The air is hot. Every diminutive, stunted shrub and every twig is hot—you would not be surprised to see them commence to smoke and burst out into flames. The earth on which we are standing is as level as a floor, and at no very remote period formed the bed of a lake of very muddy water. This lake evaporated, leaving the contained mud and condensed alkali on the surface of its bed, where it now lies as smooth, as hard and exactly resembling the "hard-finish" on a plastered wall.

Charles W. Smith, 1850   [*from* JOURNAL OF A TRIP TO CALIFORNIA]

The soil is light in color and weight, and walking through it is like

walking through ashes or slacked lime. Most of the day we were

several miles from the river and came to it but twice during the day.

I never saw such dense clouds of dust as I saw here, and it is more

disagreeable on account of it being impregnated with alkali, which

abounds in this valley. The sky is cloudless and the sun extremely

warm. We have traveled so long among the mountains, and all bear-

ing the same general appearance, that we seem to be stationary

instead of changing our position every day. In looking around me

I seem to be in a deep blue ocean of air, with the distant mountains

around as the shore.

John Muir, 1911   [*from* MY FIRST SUMMER IN THE SIERRA]

When the glorious pearl and alabaster clouds of these noonday
storms are being built I never give attention to anything else. No
mountain or mountain-range, however divinely clothed with light,
has a more enduring charm than those fleeting mountains of the
sky—floating fountains bearing water for every well, the angels of
the streams and lakes; brooding in the deep azure, or sweeping softly
along the ground over ridge and dome, over meadow, over forest,
over garden and grove; lingering with cooling shadows, refreshing
every flower, and soothing rugged rock-brows with a gentleness of
touch and gesture wholly divine.

John Muir, 1911   [*from* MY FIRST SUMMER IN THE SIERRA]

One is constantly reminded of the infinite lavishness and fertility of
Nature—inexhaustible abundance amid what seems enormous
wastage. And yet when we look into any of her operations that lie
within reach of our minds, we learn that no particle of her material
is wasted or worn out. It is eternally flowing from use to use, beauty
to yet higher beauty; and we soon cease to lament waste and death,
and rather rejoice and exult in the imperishable, unspendable wealth
of the universe, and faithfully watch and wait the reappearance of
everything that melts and fades and dies about us, feeling sure that
its next appearance will be better and more beautiful than the last.

David Rohrer Leeper, 1894   [*from* THE ARGONAUTS OF 'FORTY-NINE]

Twelve miles from Mud Lake, we entered the High Rock Canyon, which possesses some features that are unique and striking. It cuts through a range of lava that is some twenty miles in width and as bare of vegetation, as if it had cooled but the day before. The fissure or gorge that afforded us passage is about the width of a common road, and is enclosed by high walls that are carved in irregular out-line, as if by the action of an ancient ice-river.

Israel C. Russell, 1885   [*from* GEOLOGICAL HISTORY OF LAKE LAHONTAN]

As the autumn passes away, the skies lose their intense blue, and become more soft and watery, more like the skies of Italy. The hues of sunset appear richer and more varied, and during the day cloud masses trace moving lines of shadow on the surface of the desert. By and by storm-clouds gather in black, gloomy masses that envelop the ranges from base to summit. These early storm-clouds cling close to the mountains and yield to the parched deserts but a few scattered drops of rain. The observer from below hears the raging tempest amid the veiled peaks, while all about him is sun-shine. The mountains wrapped in impenetrable clouds, the glare of lightning and the deep roll of thunder as it echoes from cliff to cliff and from range to range, bring to mind the scriptural account of the storms of Sinai. And when the black clouds at last roll back from the mountains, and the sun with a wand of light dispels the storm, behold what a transfiguration! The peaks are no longer dark and somber, but glitter with the silvery sheen of freshly fallen snow.

THE ROADS *Steve Roper, 1997*

ONE LOOK AT THE ROAD SIGNS and you know you're out in nowhere. Next Services 112 Miles. Deer Crossing Next 78 Miles. Caution: Pavement Ends. Road Not Maintained by County. Road Plowed Only During Daylight Hours. Flash Flood Area: Use Caution. Road Not Maintained: Use at Own Risk. America's Loneliest Highway.

The roads are schizophrenic. Ten minutes after zooming along at seventy-five on the Interstate, you can be lurching along a sandy track, wondering which of the forks ahead to take. No signs here. Paved roads change without warning to gravel, and then to dirt. High crowns appear between the wheel tracks, and then high crowns crowned with clumps of sagebrush. Your muffler gets a free, aromatic scrubbing. It's time to turn around—if you can find a place.

For some reason, playas attract would-be Indy drivers; you can be a reckless driver for a few brief miles there, without fear of a highway patrolman. But you'd better know whether your racetrack is a wet one or a dry one. They look much the same on the surface, but one is Indy-quality and one is a trap. Sometimes the traps are obvious, for deep tire tracks mar the surface—for a short way. The in-tracks came from momentum; the out-tracks came with the help of a tow truck.

Washboard roads. Dusty roads. Roads that go fifteen miles without a single turn and barely a feature to remember. Roads that attack a mountainside and just stop—probably a mining venture that ran out of money early on. Moving plumes of dust that tell every other person in the flatlands (all three of them) of someone, friend or foe, barreling along in the distance. Probably someone coming to visit, or a rancher searching for cattle. Maybe even a tourist.

The pickup truck is the symbol of the back roads; and if you're a city person with a foreign car, you'll get a few stares. One time, in a remote parking lot, a youth pointed to my car as I approached, and I heard him exclaim to his father, "Look, Dad, a Honda!" This happened a while back, to be sure.

The barreling semitrailer truck shares the main highways with cross-country drivers. The latter, usually on I-80, are easy to spot, with their sleek cars, and their sunglasses and baseball caps strapped to their heads. Windows closed, of course; AC on. The motion of the head suggests interior music, probably loud. These drivers cling to the Interstate, stopping only two or three times in the Great Basin, happy to get moving again, westbound drivers dreaming of sophisticated San Francisco and eastbound drivers yearning for more civilized landscapes, where if you want a burger you don't have to wait an hour or two for the next town.

Elisha D. Perkins, 1850   [*from* GOLD RUSH DIARY]

No one can imagine how delightful the sight of a tree is after such
long stretches of desert, until they have tried it. We have seen very
few of any kind since leaving the Platte, and what a luxury after our
mules were taken care of, to lay down in their shade and make up
our two nights loss of sleep and hear the wind rustling their leaves
and whistling among their branches.

John Muir, 1911   [*from* MY FIRST SUMMER IN THE SIERRA]

In the more accessible ranges that stretch across the desert regions
of western Utah and Nevada, considerable numbers of Indians used
to hunt in company like packs of wolves, and being perfectly
acquainted with the topography of their hunting-grounds, and with
the habits and instincts of the game, they were pretty successful. On
the tops of nearly every one of the Nevada mountains that I have
visited, I found small, nest-like enclosures built of stones, in which,
as I afterward learned, one or more Indians would lie in wait while
their companions scoured the ridges below, knowing that the
alarmed [mountain] sheep would surely run to the summit, and
when they could be made to approach with the wind they were
shot at close range.

Joseph Wood Krutch, 1954   [*from* THE VOICE OF THE DESERT]

The eighteenth century invented a useful distinction which we have almost lost, the distinction between the beautiful and the sublime. The first, even when it escapes being merely the pretty, is easy and reassuring. The sublime, on the other hand, is touched with something which inspires awe. It is large and powerful; it carries with it the suggestion that it might overwhelm us if it would. By these definitions there is no doubt which is the right word for the desert. In intimate details, as when its floor is covered after a spring rain with the delicate little ephemeral plants, it is pretty. But such embodiments of prettiness seem to be only tolerated with affectionate contempt by the region as a whole. As a whole the desert is, in the original sense of the word, "awful." Perhaps one feels a certain boldness in undertaking to live in it and a certain pride when one discovers that one can.

Mark Twain, 1872   [*from* ROUGHING IT]

The sun beats down with dead, blistering, relentless malignity; the perspiration is welling from every pore in man and beast, but scarcely a sign of it finds its way to the surface—it is absorbed before it gets there; there is not the faintest breath of air stirring; there is not a merciful shred of cloud in all the brilliant firmament; there is not a living creature visible in any direction whither one searches the blank level that stretches its monotonous miles on every hand; there is not a sound—not a sigh—not a whisper—not a buzz, or a whir of wings, or distant pipe of bird—not even a sob from the lost souls that doubtless people that dead air.

Mary Austin, 1903 [*from* THE LAND OF LITTLE RAIN]

There are hills, rounded, blunt, burned, squeezed up out of chaos, chrome and vermilion painted, aspiring to the snow-line. Between the hills lie high level-looking plains full of intolerable sun glare, or narrow valleys drowned in a blue haze. The hill surface is streaked with ash drift and black, unweathered lava flows. After rains water accumulates in the hollows of small closed valleys, and, evaporating, leaves hard dry levels of pure desertness that get the local name of dry lakes. Where the mountains are steep and the rains heavy, the pool is never quite dry, but dark and bitter, rimmed about with the efflorescence of alkaline deposits.

John C. Frémont, 1844   [*from* REPORT OF THE EXPLORING EXPEDITION]

We were now entering a region which for us possessed a strange and extraordinary interest. We were upon the waters of the famous lake [the Great Salt Lake], which forms a salient point among the remarkable geographical features of the country and around which the vague and superstitious accounts of the trappers had thrown a delightful obscurity which we anticipated pleasure in dispelling, but which in the meantime left a crowded field for the exercise of our imagination.

Francis F. Victor, 1870   [*from* THE RIVER OF THE WEST]

The irregular hills, covered with burnt rock and scoriae; the fearful chasms, and sharp, needle-shaped rocks of its basaltic mountains; its mysterious reservoirs of water; its salt lakes and alkaline plains—[all] seem to mark it for a country uninhabitable by man and the resort only of myriads of wild-fowl, which here hatch their young in safety, and the refuge of marauding Indians, who retire here after a successful raid into the settlements. Yet it will not be left to these, for the explorer and surveyor are already traversing it everywhere, and roads are being opened in various directions.

Joseph Wood Krutch, 1954   [*from* THE VOICE OF THE DESERT]

Plants and animals are so obviously and visibly what they are because of the problems they have solved. They are part of some whole. They belong. Animals and plants, as well as men, become especially interesting when they do fit their environment, when to some extent they reveal what their response to it has been. And nowhere more than in the desert do they reveal it.

Mary Austin, 1903   [*from* THE LAND OF LITTLE RAIN]

Here are the long heavy winds and breathless calms on the tilted
mesas where dust devils dance, whirling up into a wide, pale sky.
Here you have no rain when all the earth cries for it, or quick
downpours called cloud-bursts for violence. A land of lost rivers,
with little in it to love; yet a land that once visited must be come
back to inevitably. If it were not so there would be little told of it.

Cedric Wright, 1941   [*from the* 1941 SIERRA CLUB BULLETIN]

In photography one is translating, somewhat, from one language
to another. Rock, cloud, water, and fire, in all their aura of light
and sound and depth, must be translated into the language—the
materials—of a photographic print. . . . For this, both languages
must be thoroughly felt and understood. This begins to be possible
only when one's range of dynamics and tones is that of a full-scale
keyboard, and at the fingertips. Then photography is an ample
voice, a resonant language.

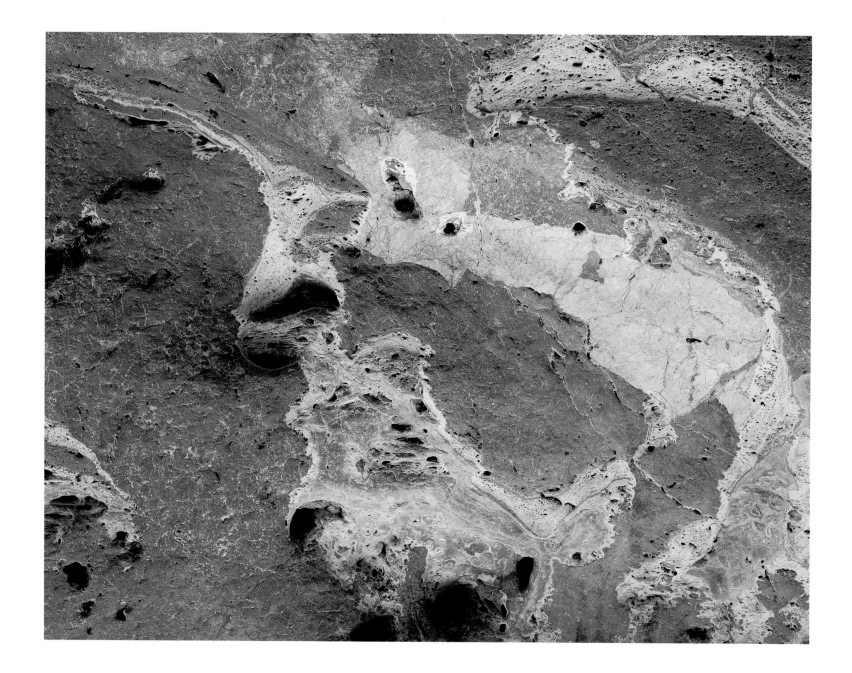

Charles W. Smith, 1850   [*from* JOURNAL OF A TRIP TO CALIFORNIA]

We crossed two high mountain ranges, with a fine stream of water
between them. In advance of us our path was filled up with mountains, one upon another. Snow to be seen. There are two classes of
mountains to be seen in this region, the largest covered with snow
and the smaller one having vegetation and filling up the space
between the others. Upon the peaks of some of the highest mountains is a stunted growth of cedar, which gives them a rather dark
appearance.

Israel C. Russell, 1885   [*from* GEOLOGICAL HISTORY OF LAKE LAHONTAN]

When the sun is high in the cloudless heavens and one is far out on the desert at a distance from rocks and trees, there is a lack of shadow and an absence of relief in the landscape that make the distance deceptive—the mountains appearing near at hand instead of leagues away—and cause one to fancy that there is no single source of light, but that the distant ranges and the desert surfaces are self-luminous. The glare of the noonday sun conceals rather than reveals the grandeur of this rugged land, but in the early morning and the near sunset the slanting light brings out mountain range after mountain range in bold relief, and reveals a world of sublimity.

Colin Fletcher, 1964   [*from* THE THOUSAND-MILE SUMMER]

By the time I reached the middle of the salt flats I understood the
paucity of pilgrims. Nothing "marked the spot." On every side
stretched a whiteness that looked level as a millpond. My feet sank
three inches into wet salt. But I stayed at the lowest point for an
hour. There was nothing to see, I suppose, except white flatness and
plunging blue mountains. But there was simplicity as well as stark-
ness. And after a while I began to hear in the silence some whisper
of the ticking aeons that had gone into making the salt and gravel
layers that went down under my feet for a thousand feet and more.
And I began to understand as well as to know that lakes had always
come and gone on the floor of the Valley—a million years here, a
million there—and that around their margins had prowled, at their
evolving times, dinosaurs and mastodons and elephants.

THE FUTURE OF THE GREAT BASIN   *Michael P. Cohen*

SOMETIME IN THE LATE AFTERNOON, you might be driving down a good two-lane road in the Great Basin with no other cars in sight. Never mind the highway sign that calls this road an extraterrestrial highway. This land is so open, so uninhabited, that it seems like the original terra firma, the skeleton and bare bones of the earth. You can see a hundred miles, across the violet shadows creeping into a long valley, to a new range of mountains and a ridgeline so mysterious and fascinating that you are surprised you have never gone there before.

Certainly the Great Basin contains more ranges of mountains than any one person can ever know; and like all ranges, each one suggests the origin of the earth. This range in front of you has such a distinctive shape you are sure you have never seen it before; but while you have driven this road scores of times, you have never seen the geography revealed in this light. You stop the car, consult the map, and realize that you were walking up a canyon on the other side of the ridge only a few months ago.

Set apart by a distinctive geology and biogeography, and scarred by its recent human history, this region tests human perception, tricks human memory, and divines human desire. The past five decades of human behavior here include ultimate human horrors, yet this land has been inhabited for a much longer time by the human cultures and the biota that preceded those modern humans who have recently turned it to their own strange military needs.

Modern Americans have been here for such a short time, have experienced such a limited range of conditions, have asked such paltry questions! Coming here in the midst of an interglacial era, what they have seen in the Great Basin is a forbidding climate, a cold desert, some exposed minerals, a few shrubs and grasses, and an empty space. Not long ago, a paleoecologist patiently explained a simple fact to me: The earth has spent 90 percent of the last two million years in glacial eras; and during those times, the Great Basin's valleys and mountains were the home of alpine forests. These two million years probably included about ten complete climate cycles, so the present climate thus represents only about 10 percent of recent history. Our era, in other words, is neither representative nor final.

Add the following fact: Modern humans have been on this earth for about 100,000 years; they have inhabited the earth through less than half of one glacial cycle. The evidence of modern humans in the Great Basin is certain from only some 11,500 years ago. This understanding is relevant to any future we might imagine for the region or ourselves.

Because the Great Basin seems to be mostly empty space, its future has been highly contested; it has been claimed most recently by traditional patterns of exploitation. The booming and busting mining eras of the last 150 years have left, and are still creating, monuments to a simple theory of history—that people find only what they seek, asking narrow economic questions and receiving limited answers. The ranching history of the past century leaves its own legacy of conflict between memory and desire, and after permanently altering the grasslands of the region, ranching continues to hang on as a marginal occupation. The military history here has been the most dramatic and most recent, a textbook case of the human mind confronting empty space as a repository of its worst nightmares. The concept of the Great Basin as a patchwork of bombing ranges, nuclear reserves, and secret installations comes from the earliest understanding of the region as a place of no exit, where everything flows in and nothing flows out. Proponents of the MX missile system of the early 1980s, in the ultimate expression of this idea, wanted to make the entire region a nuclear target capable of absorbing the weaponry of an evil empire.

The Great Basin is not an empty repository, but an archive of natural and human history full of all the wonderful and horrible things that make it a stark and complete picture of the world and of human ingenuity at work on the world. The results of military occupation must be preserved, but the real and viable future for the region resides in its natural history and natural beauty. An open and visible geology makes each mountain range a textbook for the study not only of the discipline itself, but of the meaning of geology as space.

The region's biological history has its own fascination. Here, for instance, bristlecone pines, the world's oldest living trees, grow at high altitudes on limestone ranges. The tree rings of old bristlecones, living and dead, embody ten thousand years of natural history; the forests are also an archive, a window into the climatic history of the entire postglacial era. These trees provide a record of terrestrial conditions that is of the same temporal span as human occupation. The bristlecone has, in the past forty years, acquired an additional value as modern sculpture, and the old groves are now preserved as exquisite and priceless sculpture gardens.

Here is what we might have learned, late in the twentieth century, from our recent devaluation of nuclear weapons and our reevaluation of bristlecone pines: A portion of the earth thought a desolate wasteland by one ignorant generation can become highly valued by the next, if the next generation grows wiser. The Great Basin is, at this very moment, on the cusp of such a transition of thought. Nobody would imagine this region to be an Eden, yet it no longer seems a desolate wasteland. We begin to notice that it is full of things that make it what it is. People come here in increasing numbers, attracted by its beauty, but hardly knowing yet what attracts them.

TECHNICAL NOTES

I made 154 photographs for this book over a period of time beginning on June 20, 1987, and ending on December 31, 1996. The photos were made with a Gowland 4 x 5 view camera and lenses of 150mm, 210mm, and 300mm focal lengths. Transparency film was used for all but two of the photographs. No filters were used other than a standard ultraviolet and haze filter.

A NOTE FROM EVERCOLOR FINE ART

The goal of EverColor Fine Art is to produce and present the finest photographic prints possible. The photographers that we represent are serious and committed artists whose work is careful, considered, and only of the highest quality.

Therefore, we are pleased to make available exquisite prints of Mr. Fiddler's work from this book. The prints are made using EverColor's proprietary pigment transfer and dye print processes. By combining advanced digital imaging with the time-honored transfer process, EverColor is capable of making prints that exhibit rich, deep colors, needlepoint sharpness, and a luminescence that captures the ephemeral qualities of mood and lighting.

All of our limited-edition prints are signed by the artist.

We invite you to call EverColor Fine Art (1-800-533-5050) for more information.